Reena's Bollywood Dream: A Story About Sexual Abuse

By: Jewel Kats
Illustrated by Richa Kinra

from the Growing With Love Series

Loving Healing Press

Library of Congress Cataloging-in-Publication Data

Kats, Jewel, 1978-
Reena's Bollywood dream: a story about sexual abuse / by Jewel Kats.
p. cm. – (Growing with love series)
ISBN-13: 978-1-61599-014-6 (trade paper : alk. paper)
ISBN-10: 1-61599-014-3 (trade paper : alk. paper)
1. Child sexual abuse – Juvenile literature. 2. Sexually abused girls – Juvenile literature. I. Title.
HV6570.K38 2010
362.76 – dc22
2009037554

Published by
Loving Healing Press
5145 Pontiac Trail
Ann Arbor, MI 48105

www.LHPress.com
info@LHPress.com
Tollfree 888-761-6268
Fax 734-663-6861

Loving Healing Press

Distributed by: New Leaf Distributing, Ingram Book Group, Bertrams Books

DEDICATION

For Mom, Dad, Masi, Nidhi, Sharad, Gagan
and especially, Roopali

❁ ❁ ❁

GLOSSARY

Nani means grandma. To be exact it means your mom's mother.

Masala are spices used to flavor food or tea.

Tandoori chicken is a hot food item served at lunch or dinner.

Lengha is an Indian outfit worn by girls and women. It has two main pieces, which are a blouse and a long skirt.

"Look who's here, Reena!" Nani shouted.

I almost knocked over my grandma and parents as I raced to the front doors. I wiggled past the crowd. And then I saw my uncle.

I tackled him into a bear hug. "You look just like your photographs, Uncle Jessi!"

"Reena!" Daddy remarked gruffly. "You're not showing respect to your elders."

Uncle Jessi held me close. "It's okay, there's no need to scold her," he said. "Reena and I are old pen pals."

Uncle Jessi ruffled my curls. "I've brought a treat for you." He reached into his fall jacket and pulled out a DVD.

I threw my arms into the air. "It's a Bollywood movie!"

I watched my uncle's cab driver huff and puff as he dragged in four large suitcases.

"I packed thirty years worth of memories from India," Uncle Jessi told me.

I couldn't imagine what it'd be like to tuck away eight years of my life into a matching luggage set.

Once everything was put aside, the grownups enjoyed hot masala tea. Meanwhile, I danced away to Indian movie songs.

Nani looked at Uncle Jessi. "Welcome to this great country, son. I hope you enjoy your new home."

"You really are lucky," I said with a twirl. "Now you have the chance to watch an American girl like me dance to Bollywood music."

I copied every groovy move of the Indian actress on our TV screen.

"How do I look?" I asked, while my hips shook.

"You look ridiculous, Reena," Mommy snapped.

I wiped my now-sticky brow. "But Mommy, you know I want to be a Bollywood star when I grow up."

"We've talked about this before," Mommy said. "Nice Indian girls — and that's who you are — don't grow up to become actresses."

Daddy cleared his throat. "You're from a family of doctors, Reena," he said. "You should be following in the footsteps of your parents, not the dance steps of some silly actress."

I went to my bedroom and doodled in my notebook for a while. I only got up after I had a sniff of tandoori spices coming from the kitchen. I followed my nose.

"Hey, Reena!" Uncle Jessi called from his bedroom. "Come here."

I hopped over the unzipped suitcase that blocked his door. "Yeah?"

He placed a heavy envelope in my hand.

I peeked inside. I couldn't believe it. "My letters!" I cried. "You kept everything I wrote to you?"

"Of course," he answered. "Your written thoughts are way too special to throw away."

My eyes twinkled.

A few days later, I found a note stuck to my bathroom mirror. I forgot all about brushing my teeth.

"I've planned a surprise for you," the note read. "Meet me in my bedroom at four o'clock sharp. This is our little secret. Nobody will be home then. Signed, your pen pal."

I tucked the letter into my PJ pocket and stared at my ticking watch. "Geez, it's only time for breakfast!" I exclaimed with a sigh.

At long last, four o'clock rolled around.

"You're right on time!" Uncle Jessi laughed. "Did everyone leave for the shopping trip?"

"Yeah, the whole family's gone," I said, breathless. "Now don't keep me waiting any longer! What's the surprise?"

"Look under my bed."

I dropped down on all fours. I yanked out a gift wrapped box.

"What's inside?" I gave the present a good shake. I heard a soft jingling sound.

"Go ahead and open it."

I tore at the red tissue wrap in a snap. I found glass bangles, silver anklets with the tiniest of bells, and an itty-bitty violet blouse with a matching lengha skirt.

"This outfit is fancy enough for an Indian actress!" I gushed.

My uncle smiled. "You got it."

Reena's Bollywood Dream

"Why don't you try everything on?" Uncle Jessi urged me.

I looked around his overstuffed room. "But where will I change?"

"You can change right where you are." He turned his back. "Meanwhile I'll get the next surprise ready."

As I slipped into my lengha's puffy skirt, I saw Uncle Jessi smile at me through the mirror of his dresser. This time I turned around.

"I'm all dressed," I announced.

Uncle Jessi walked over, and stood right in front of me. He was breathing awfully hard. "Let me take a good look at you."

Suddenly I felt like there wasn't enough fabric covering my tummy, arms, or back. I'd never worn a blouse cut like this before.

"My, my," he whistled. "You're more gorgeous than any movie star I know."

"Really?" I giggled. "Nobody's ever said that to me before."

"I mean it," Uncle Jessi said. "Honest."

I stared at myself in the mirror of Uncle Jessi's dresser. "This lengha is really special. Where did you get it?"

"I made it with my own hands," he said.

Now I was super surprised. "Men can actually sew?"

"Guys and girls can do anything they put their minds to," he said. "And this includes you."

Uncle Jessi went to his closet, and pulled out a video camera and a stand. "Now I'm going to turn you into a Bollywood actress."

My eyeballs popped. "How will you do that?"

"Simple." He started to play Indian music. "You see, I'll pretend to be a director, and you'll pretend to be a movie star."

"How cool!" I shouted.

12

I danced my heart out. My legs and arms moved like magic. The music pumped right through me.

"Shake your hips more," Uncle Jessi said.

Like a good actress I did.

"Throw your hair around," Uncle Jessi said.

Like a good actress I did.

"Widen your smile, Reena," Uncle Jessi said.

Like a good actress I did.

"We're going for a different look now," Uncle Jessi declared. "Keep moving to the music, but I want you to look more simple."

I nodded my head. "Okay. I get it, Mr. Director."

"Start by removing your bangles," he instructed.

I shook off my bangles while my wrists twisted to the Bollywood beat.

"You're doing well," Uncle Jessi said. "Now get rid of your anklets."

I stomped my feet wildly to the music and my anklets flew off.

"Nice drama, Reena," Uncle Jessi said. "This time free yourself from your blouse."

I STOPPED MOVING TOTALLY.

"I can't do that," I said. "I'm not wearing anything under my blouse."

Uncle Jessi ground his teeth. "Reena, I'm the director — do as I say."

I crossed my arms tightly. "I don't like this game anymore."

My uncle shoved his video camera into its stand. The red recording light blinked like never before. He grabbed onto my arm. My sweaty hand slipped from his grip.

I broke free, and ran out of his bedroom door. I shouted: "HELP!" at the top of my lungs to empty hallways. I practically flew upstairs.

I heard the front door slam behind Uncle Jessi. He had left me home alone!

I locked myself in my bedroom, and tore off my uncle's stupid lengha. I kicked it around. I watched the fabric rip apart. I finally changed into my PJs. I laid in bed with watery eyes. *Will my family even believe what's happened?* As I turned onto my side, I heard a crinkling sound from my PJ pocket. I pulled out the surprise letter Uncle Jessi left for me in the bathroom. I jumped up. That's it! I needed proof!

Even though nobody was home, I was extra careful and tiptoed to my uncle's room. I went to his video camera stand and pulled out the tape he recorded of me. As I zipped out of his room, my parents and Nani walked in the front door.

"Family! There's something terrible you need to see!" I said, and ran towards them with fresh tears.

My family was shocked when I showed them the tape and the letter.

"I'm proud of you, Reena," Daddy said. "You did the right thing by telling us. You could've also told another grownup you trusted, like your teacher."

"Parts of your body that get covered by a bathing suit are private," Mommy added. "Nobody should ask to see them. You made the right choice by saying 'no.'"

"We would've believed you regardless," Nani said, loud and clear. "Now we'll contact the police."

Some nights I have awful dreams. I have found it helpful to talk with my family and a therapist who is helping me deal with my feelings.

I also haven't given up on my dream to become an actress. My parents gave me permission to join the drama club at school. Tonight's my first performance. As I walk onto stage, I see my parents and Nani sitting upfront. I smile because I know my uncle's not in the audience.

AUTHOR BIOGRAPHY

Jewel Kats (1978 –) is an award-winning writer. For six years, she penned a teen advice column for **Young People's Press**. "Confidentially Yours" appeared in dozens of newspapers via the **Scripps Howard News Service** and **TorStar Syndication Services**. Her work on this column led her to win a $5,000 writing scholarship by women's publisher, **Harlequin Enterprises Ltd**. She later earned a $15,000 scholarship from **Global Television Network**. Jewel's upcoming books include: *Cinderella's Magical Wheelchair* and *What Do You Use to Help Your Body?* She hails from an Indo-Canadian background, and calls Toronto home.

Jewel's website: www.JewelKats.com
Contact info: JK@JewelKats.com

Richa Kinra (1984 –) is the internationally published illustrator of several children's books, adult fiction books and spiritual poems. Her books include titles such as *Annabelle's Secret: A Story About Sexual Abuse, Will the Courageous: A Story About Sexual Abuse, Debra meets her best friend in Kindergarten.* She is from India. She lives with her family, and says she received a lot of encouragement from her parents and friends who saw her artistic talent. Apart from children book illustrations she has also freelanced for various magazines and websites. Her hand painted works are primarily in watercolors, acrylic and oils, sometimes incorporating colored pencil, dry colors, pen & ink and/or collage.

Richa's Website: http://www.coroflot.com/pinkdamselblack
Contact Info: richa.kinra@gmail.com

Camp CADI for Girls!

Imagine a place where survivors of childhood sexual abuse (CSA) can reclaim the joy of childhood. Imagine a place where they can find confidence through the power of choice, find healing through the power of art and find hope through the power of community. Imagine Camp CADI!

Created by *Safe Girls Strong Girls* founder Amy Barth, Camp CADI (Irish for "simple happiness") is the first of its kind, offering CSA survivors ages 8 to 21 a unique opportunity to enjoy the fun-filled, memorable moments that only a true camp experience can provide. For one week, in the playful, exciting and safe environment of Camp Twin Lakes, girls get to be girls again!

Camp Activities

Camp CADI includes traditional camp activities such as swimming, canoeing, mountain biking, fishing, campfires, and sleeping under the stars. We also include a creative mix of art therapy and experiential learning programs to complete our retreat. Campers develop confidence-boosting skills during interactive experiential learning workshops, while rediscovering their own voice through music, drama, storytelling, journaling and other arts related activities.

Throughout the week, the girls discover that they are not alone, realize the abuse was not their fault, and learn that community fellowship can be a great healer as they build trusting relationships with their camp peers and counselors.

"Camp CADI has really helped me deal with my sexual abuse by helping me rebuild my confidence and find my own inner strength. Being able to form friendships with other survivors of sexual abuse has shown me that I am not alone in my struggles and that each one of us is beautiful and we should not be ashamed of our abuse. Camp CADI really helped me get my life ontrack and gave me back the most valuable thing for a survivor: hope. Camp has truly changed my life forever and I hope that it will continue to change other young survivors lives as well."

www.CampCadi.com

Other great titles in the Growing With Love Series

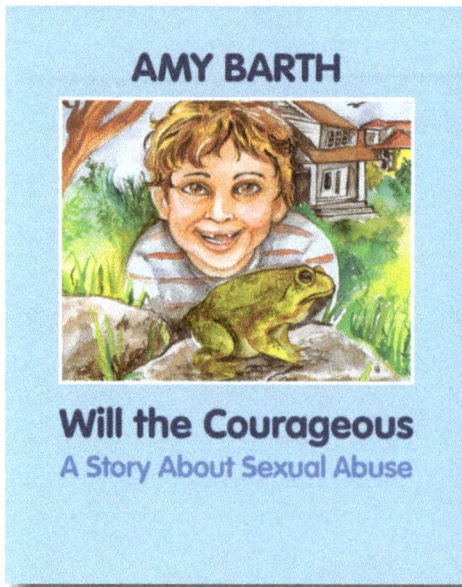

AMY BARTH

Will the Courageous
A Story About Sexual Abuse

Will is a typical six-year-old boy. Will enjoys having his Nana as a babysitter. Recently, Nana's cousin Perry has come to visit and suddenly Will no longer wants to go there. He starts having nightmares, acting out in school and wetting his bed. Will's parents are worried. What is wrong with Will?

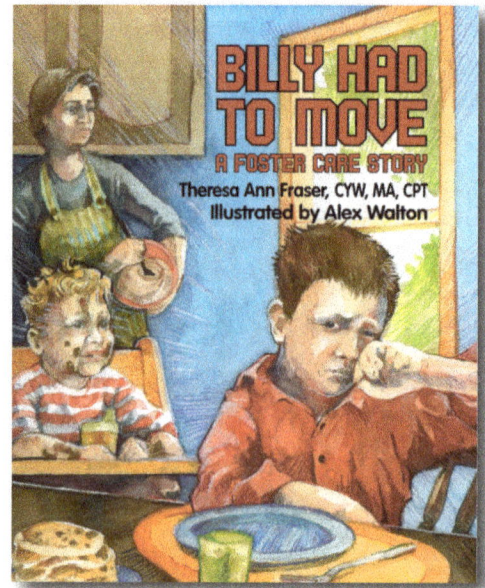

BILLY HAD TO MOVE
A FOSTER CARE STORY
Theresa Ann Fraser, CYW, MA, CPT
Illustrated by Alex Walton

Child Protection Services have been involved with Billy an his mother for some time now. He has been happily settle with his grandmother. As the story unfolds, Billy's grand mother has unexpectedly passed away.

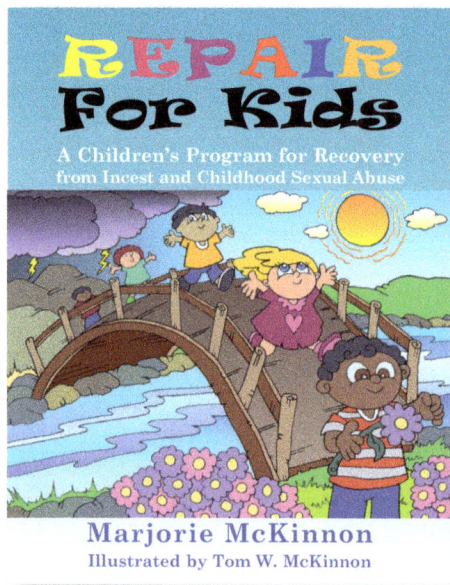

REPAIR For Kids
A Children's Program for Recovery from Incest and Childhood Sexual Abuse
Marjorie McKinnon
Illustrated by Tom W. McKinnon

"*REPAIR for Kids* provides a comprehensive, honest and passionate approach for children recovering from sexual abuse. Children will benefit from this book, and be encouraged to continue on their recovery journey."

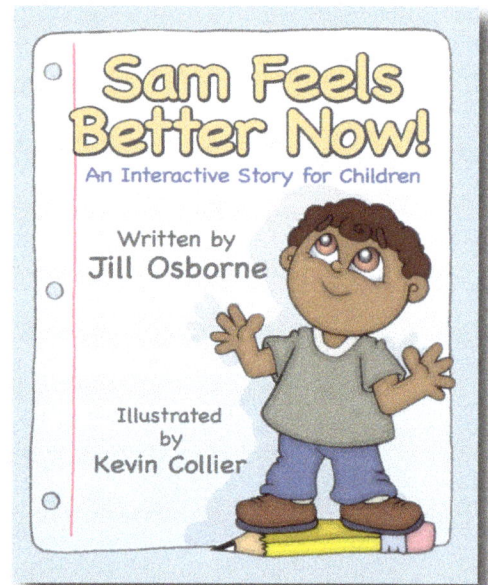

Sam Feels Better Now!
An Interactive Story for Children
Written by
Jill Osborne

Illustrated by
Kevin Collier

Sam saw something awful and scary! Ms. Carol, a specia therapist, will show Sam how to feel better. Children can help Sam feel better too by using drawings, play, and storytelling activities.

...from Loving Healing Press
www.LHPress.com

Books for Caregivers and Therapists too!

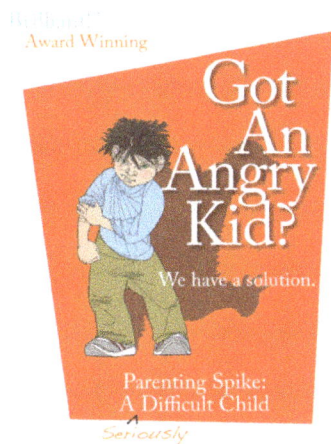

Got An Angry Kid?

Booklist Award Winning

Got An Angry Kid?

We have a solution.

Parenting Spike: A Seriously Difficult Child

by Andrew D. Gibson, Ph.D.

Does your family live in conflict? Does your child have a psychiatric label (such as ADHD, oppositional defiance, conduct disorder, bi-polar disorder) or the behavior that would get him/her one? Have you lost (or nearly lost) control of your child? If you answered YES to any of these three things, then *ACT* can help you as it has helped thousands of other families restore love and integrity to their relationships!

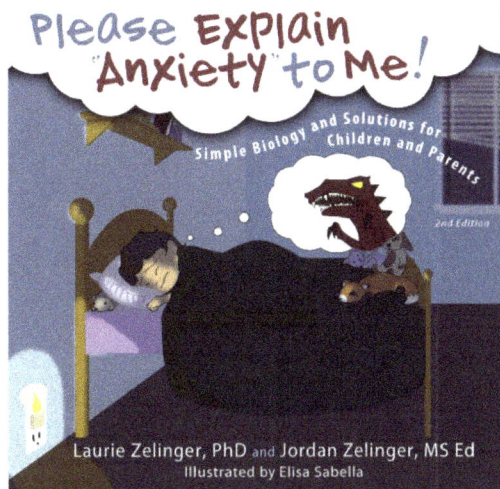

Please Explain "Anxiety" to Me!

Please Explain "Anxiety" to Me!

Simple Biology and Solutions for Children and Parents

2nd Edition

Laurie Zelinger, PhD and Jordan Zelinger, MS Ed
Illustrated by Elisa Sabella

This book translates anxiety from the jargon of psychology into concrete experiences that children can relate to. Children and their parents will understand the biological and emotional components of anxiety responsible for the upsetting symptoms they experience. *Please Explain...* gives accurate physiological information in child friendly language

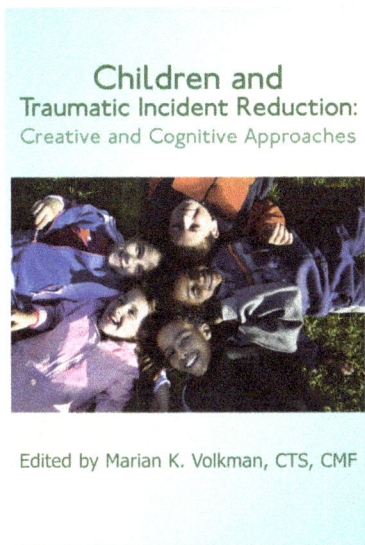

Children and Traumatic Incident Reduction

Children and Traumatic Incident Reduction: Creative and Cognitive Approaches

Edited by Marian K. Volkman, CTS, CMF

What if we could resolve childhood trauma fully, gently, and completely while the child is still young?

We Can. Read *Children and Traumatic Incident Reduction* and find out how!

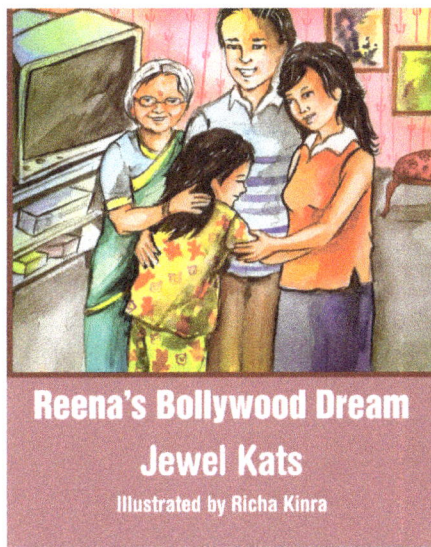

Reena's Bollywood Dream

Reena's Bollywood Dream

Jewel Kats

Illustrated by Richa Kinra

Uncle Jessi has just emigrated from India to America, and is a welcome addition to her family household. Uncle Jessi and Reena are old pen pals, and he recognizes her desperation to become a Bollywood actress. One day, Uncle Jessi plans a secret surprise. He invites her to take part in a pretend acting game. Reena jumps at the chance.

...from Loving Healing Press
www.LHPress.com

www.ingramcontent.com/pod-product-compliance
Lightning Source LLC
Chambersburg PA
CBHW061412090426
42741CB00021B/3487